Darcy Mellinger, M.A.T., NBCT

Publishing Credits

Corinne Burton, M.A.Ed., *President and Publisher*
Emily R. Smith, M.A.Ed., *SVP of Content Development*
Véronique Bos, *Vice President of Creative*
Lynette Ordoñez, *Content Manager*
Avery Wickersham, *Assistant Editor*
Jill Malcolm, *Graphic Designer*

Standards

NGSS Lead States. 2013. *Next Generation Science Standards: For States, By States*. Washington, DC: The National Academies Press.
© 2022 TESOL International Association
© 2022 Board of Regents of the University of Wisconsin System

Image Credits: p.97 Jill Malcolm; p.98 Jill Malcolm; p.110 (top center) Shutterstock/Dziewul; p.121 (top center) Shutterstock/Nils Versemann; p.122 Shutterstock/Opachevsky Irina; p.148 (top left) Shutterstock Piu_Piu; p.159 (top left) Shutterstock/Johnnie Rik; p.159 (top center) Shutterstock/OAnderson; p.160 (top left) Shutterstock/Delpixel; p.160 (top right) Shutterstock/Alex Boutte; p.162 (top left) Shutterstock Bob Pool; p.182 (top left) Shutterstock/Wangkun Jia; p.182 (top center) Shutterstock/miker; p.182 (top right) Shutterstock/Leonard Zhukovsky; all other images Shutterstock and/or iStock

A division of Teacher Created Materials
5482 Argosy Avenue
Huntington Beach, CA 92649
www.tcmpub.com/shell-education
ISBN 978-1-0876-6267-1
© 2023 Shell Educational Publishing, Inc.
Printed in China 51497

Table of Contents

What Do the Experts Say?

Welcome to *180 Days of Science for Prekindergarten*! Three strands of science—physical science, life science, and Earth and space science—are introduced and explored throughout this book. Students will have the opportunity to learn and show what they know about science topics. The activities in this book provide students practice in the foundational knowledge and analytical skills to better understand the world around them. Students are encouraged to investigate their own environment to make meaningful connections to new science concepts.

Foundations

Learning foundational science skills will help students be better prepared for science in kindergarten. It is estimated that 85–90 percent of brain growth occurs in the first five years of life (First Things First 2017). Science is the study of the physical and natural world through observation and experiments. Not only is it important for students to learn scientific facts, it is also important for them to develop a desire for new knowledge.

Early childhood researchers and educators uphold the following principles and approaches in their work with young children:

- Exploring the natural world is an important part of childhood. Science can be viewed as a process of constructing, understanding, and developing ideas. It is a natural focus for early childhood programs (Worth 2010). In this book, students are invited to explore the natural world around them.

- Students need structured science experiences that are supported by teachers. These opportunities should cover the same sets of ideas over time (Duschl, Schweingruber, and Shouse 2007). In *180 Days of Science for Prekindergarten*, students will engage in structured content from each strand of science.

- Science is a social endeavor. Working with a community and using scientific tools to represent scientific ideas leads to proficiency (Michaels, Shouse, and Schweingruber 2007). Across the pages of this book, children have opportunities to socially interact with peers or adults to learn about science concepts and share thoughts and ideas with others.

In *180 Days of Science for Prekindergarten*, a yearlong plan is mapped out strategically to place importance on science content for prekindergarten learners.

What Do the Experts Say? *(cont.)*

The Need for Practice

To be successful in science, students must understand how people interact with the physical world. They not only master scientific practices but also learn how to look at the world with curiosity and inquiry. Through repeated practice, students will learn how a variety of factors affect the world in which they live. Students will develop the confidence to apply the critical-thinking skills needed to apply and test scientific knowledge. Learning science throughout this year will be filled with awe and wonder as children investigate the world around them.

Practice Pages

180 Days of Science for Prekindergarten offers teachers and parents a full page of science practice for each day of the school year. Every practice page provides content, questions, and activities that are directly related to science topics and standards. These activities introduce and reinforce grade-level skills across a variety of high-interest science concepts. The content and questions are easy to prepare and implement as part of the daily routine. Regardless of how the pages are used, students will be engaged in practicing the foundational skills to learn science through these standards-based activities.

Students are also given the opportunity to extend their learning. Throughout the book, children are encouraged to incorporate the arts into their learning. Students may act, dance, sing, and draw to express their new understandings of scientific concepts. The practice pages in *180 Days of Science for Prekindergarten* are designed to awaken student interest through multiple pathways of experience.

What Do the Experts Say? *(cont.)*

Standards-Based Instruction

The science skills included in *180 Days of Science for Prekindergarten* are aligned to standards (see pages 12–14). This book is organized into three sections based on the three science strands: physical science, life science, and Earth and space science.

In the **Physical Science** section, students learn about and experiment with pushes and pulls. They look at types of interactions, such as speed and colliding. Students examine the relationships between forces and design their own projects. Next, students learn about the effects of sunlight on Earth. They also consider reducing the warming effect of sunlight in different settings.

When students investigate **Life Science**, they explore the amazing living things on our planet and how they interact. Students learn about plants and animals and what they need to survive. Then, children investigate the interdependence of organisms. Students examine the traits of young plants and animals and how they are similar to the traits of their parents. Students compare living and nonliving things and take a deeper look at the parts of different types of animals. Finally, students learn about life cycles.

In the third section, students learn about **Earth and Space Science**. First, students learn about Earth systems and different types of weather and climates. Learners also examine the ways in which plants, animals, and humans change the environment. Children discover types of severe weather and how weather forecasting can help people prepare for such weather. Finally, students examine ways to reduce human impact on Earth. A matching game called *Taking Care of the Earth* is provided in the Digital Resources to reinforce the concept that we can reduce our impact on Earth.

Diagnostic Assessment

In addition to providing opportunities for frequent practice, teachers and parents must be able to assess student understanding of science concepts, big ideas, vocabulary, and reasoning. It is important to effectively find and address student misconceptions and gaps, build on their current understandings, and challenge their thinking at appropriate levels. Assessment is a long-term process that involves careful analysis of student responses from a multitude of sources. This may include discussions, projects, and practice sheets. This book provides a rubric to evaluate student responses on the activity sheets.

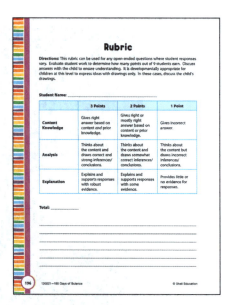

How to Use This Book

Using the Practice Pages

The practice pages in this book provide instructional opportunities for each of the 180 days of the school year. Activities are organized into three sections—Physical Science, Life Science, and Earth and Space Science. Each day's science skills are aligned to standards that may be found on pages 12–14 in this book.

Easy-to-follow directions help adults support students as they complete activities.

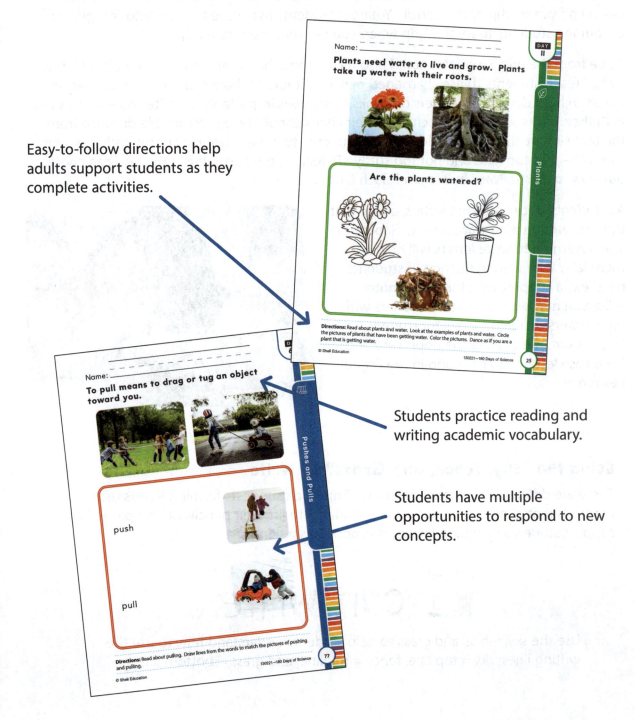

Students practice reading and writing academic vocabulary.

Students have multiple opportunities to respond to new concepts.

How to Use This Book (cont.)

Letter Formation and Proper Pencil Grip

When students write throughout the pages of this book, encourage proper pencil grip. It is important for children to learn how to properly grip their pencils early. Students will naturally find their dominant hand. If a student writes with both their right and their left hand, brain research indicates that it is preferred to allow them to write with both hands. The best pencil grip for children is with their pointer finger on the top, thumb on the side, and three fingers below the pencil to support the grip. The grip of the pencil is about one inch from the tip of the pencil. Younger students may have to grow into this grip, so encourage students to try this grip when you see that they are ready.

Aside from the grip, students should also have proper habits and environment in which to write. Teach students to use sharpened pencils. Students should use their nondominant hands to hold down their papers or books. Posture is important, so invite students to sit tall with their backs supported by chairs. Their chairs should be a comfortable distance from the table where they are working. Teach students to press down on pencils with medium strength—not too hard and not too softly. To learn more about this topic, you can check out *How to Hold a Pencil* by Megan Hirsch (2010).

As students trace and write letters, check that they are writing letters accurately. Repetition when learning to write letters will help them later with writing fluency. If students need extra support with their fine-motor skills, you may want to write the letters with highlighters or light markers for students to trace. Examples of all of the uppercase and lowercase letters can be found in the Digital Resources.

Using the "Sky, Fence, and Grass" to Write

There are different ways to write letters. This book suggests forming letters using methods that generally do not require students to lift their pencils off the page. To support students in writing letters, this book has writing.

Use the sky, fence, and grass to help students understand how to use the writing lines: sky = top line, fence = midline, and grass = bottom line.

Activities Overview

Over the 180 days of learning, students will begin to examine physical science, life science, and Earth and space science. The following activities are used throughout this book as students explore science topics.

Time to Draw	Children draw and color pictures to explain what they learned or have experienced.
Matching	Learners draw lines between related concepts.
Multiple-Choice Questions	Students circle the best choices to answer questions.
Color-by-Number	Children color sections of an image based on a coloring key.
Dot-to-Dot	Students connect the dots to make an image related to a science concept.
Sequencing	Children put the steps of a process in correct, sequential order.
Word Search	Children hunt in word searches to find the academic vocabulary.
Write Words	Students trace and write academic vocabulary to show their understandings of scientific concepts.
Design, Engineer, and Build	Children apply their scientific knowledge by designing and building projects to experiment with and show what they have learned.

Assessment and Diagnosis

Determine Baseline

When assessing student progress in early childhood, it is important to consider children's developmental levels in all learning domains. Determining each child's or the whole class's baseline can guide instruction in both pacing and depth. You may also want to determine whether a child or class needs additional support in a content area. When a child or class excels in a content area, it is best to stretch student learning to a higher level of instruction. In that case, you may wish to enrich the learning with additional materials. See the suggested websites on page 201 of this book and the activities in the Digital Resources for ideas to extend and enrich learning.

Progress Monitoring

Formal or diagnostic assessments may be conducted periodically—often once a semester or trimester. You may also prefer to administer pre- and post-assessments. It is excellent practice to assess students at the beginning, middle, and end of the year. Another way progress may be monitored is at the beginning and end of each of the three strands— physical science, life science, and Earth and space science. Teachers and parents are encouraged to collaborate with teams, schools, and other parents to determine what is best for your learners. These formal assessments are used to determine whether a child is thriving with the curriculum or if changes are needed to meet the child's needs.

Assessment and Diagnosis *(cont.)*

Rubric and Recording Sheets

When analyzing data, it is important for teachers and parents to reflect on how their teaching practices influenced students' responses and to identify areas where additional instruction may be needed. Essentially, the data gathered from assessments will be used to inform instruction: to slow down, to continue as planned, to speed up, or to reteach in a new way.

You may use the practice pages as formative assessments of the key science strands. The rubric and recording pages included in this book allow you to quickly score students' work and monitor their progress on the written response assignments (see pages 196–199 in this book and in the Digital Resources). The answer key on pages 202–206 provides answers for the written, matching, and multiple-choice response questions. The rubric may be used for any open-ended questions where student responses vary.

It is developmentally appropriate at this level for a child to express ideas with drawings only. It may be helpful to review the Stages of Emergent Writing (Byington and Kim 2017) and to analyze and track student progress. In these cases, you will want to discuss the child's written response to ensure you understand what the child was expressing in drawings.

After the last day of practice (Day 180), you may use the certificate on page 195 or in the Digital Resources to celebrate students' learning achievements.

Standards Correlations

Shell Education is committed to producing educational materials that are research and standards based. To support this effort, this resource is correlated to the academic standards of all 50 states, the District of Columbia, the Department of Defense Dependent Schools, and the Canadian provinces. A correlation is also provided for key professional educational organizations.

To print a customized correlation report for your state, please visit our website at **www.tcmpub.com/administrators/correlations** and follow the online directions. If you require assistance in printing correlation reports, please contact the Customer Service Department at 1-800-858-7339.

NGSS Standards and State Themes

The activities in this book are aligned to the following Next Generation Science Standards (NGSS):

	Science Topic	NGSS and State Standards
Life Science	Plants	All organisms have external parts. Plants also have different parts (roots, stems, leaves, flowers, fruits) that help them survive and grow. Plants need water and light to grow.
	Animals	All organisms have external parts. Different animals use their body parts in different ways to see, hear, grasp objects, protect themselves, move from place to place, and seek, find, and take in food, water, and air. All animals need food in order to live and grow. They obtain their food from plants or from other animals. Animals have body parts that capture and convey different kinds of information needed for growth and survival. Animals respond to these inputs with behaviors that help them survive.
	Traits	Develop a model to describe the fact that some young plants and animals are similar to, but not exactly like, their parents.
	Living and Nonliving	Plants and animals have basic needs and depend on the living and nonliving things around them for survival. Differentiate between living and nonliving things based upon whether they have basic needs and produce offspring. Sort plants and animals into groups based on physical characteristics such as color, size, body covering, or leaf shape. Identify basic parts of plants and animals.
	Life Cycle of a Plant	Observe changes that are part of a simple life cycle of a plant: seed, seedling, plant, flower, and fruit.

Standards Correlations (cont.)

	Science Topic	NGSS and State Standards
Physical Science	Pushes and Pulls	Plan and conduct an investigation to compare the effects of different strengths or directions of pushes and pulls on the motion of an object. Analyze data to determine if a design solution works as intended to change the speed or direction of an object with a push or a pull. Pushes and pulls can have different strengths and directions. Pushing or pulling on an object can change the speed or direction of its motion and can start or stop it.
	Interactions	When objects touch or collide, they push on one another and can change motion.
	Energy and Forces	A bigger push or pull makes things speed up or slow down more quickly. A situation that people want to change or create can be approached as a problem to be solved through engineering. Such problems may have many acceptable solutions.
	Sunlight's Effect on Earth	Make observations to determine the effect of sunlight on Earth's surface. Sunlight warms Earth's surface.
	Reducing Warming Effect of Sunlight	Use tools and materials to design and build a structure that will reduce the warming effect of sunlight on an area.
Earth and Space Science	Weather and Climate	Weather is the combination of sunlight, wind, snow, or rain, and temperature in a particular region at a particular time. People measure these conditions to describe and record the weather and to notice patterns over time. Use and share observations of local weather conditions to describe patterns over time.
	Changing Environments	Plants and animals can change their environment. Construct an argument supported by evidence for how plants and animals (including humans) can change the environment to meet their needs. Things that people do to live comfortably can affect the world around them. But they can make choices that reduce their impacts on the land, water, air, and other living things.
	Needs of Plants, Animals, and People	Use a model to represent the relationship between the needs of different plants or animals (including humans) and the places they live.

Standards Correlations (cont.)

	Science Topic	NGSS and State Standards
Earth and Space Science	Weather Forecasting	Ask questions to obtain information about the purpose of weather forecasting to prepare for, and respond to, severe weather.
		Some kinds of severe weather are more likely than others in a given region. Weather scientists forecast severe weather so that the communities can prepare for and respond to these events.
	Reducing Human Impact	Communicate solutions that will reduce the impact of humans on the land, water, air, and/or other living things in the local environment.
		Living things need water, air, and resources from the land, and they live in places that have the things they need. Humans use natural resources for everything they do.
		Things that people do to live comfortably can affect the world around them. But they can make choices that reduce their impacts on the land, water, air, and other living things.
		Asking questions, making observations, and gathering information are helpful in thinking about problems.
		Designs can be conveyed through sketches, drawings, or physical models. These representations are useful in communicating ideas for a problem's solutions to other people.

WIDA Standards

In this book, the following English language development standards are met:

- Standard 1: English language learners communicate for social and instructional purposes within the school setting.

- Standard 4: English language learners communicate information, ideas and concepts necessary for academic success in the content area of science.

Name: _____

A seed is the part of a plant that can grow a new plant.

Time to Draw

Directions: Read about seeds. Find seeds in your home, in books, or in nature. Notice how the seeds are alike and different. Draw different kinds of seeds you find.

Name: _____

A seedling is a young plant grown from a seed.

Plants

Time to Draw

I see seedlings.

Directions: Read about seedlings. Find seedlings in your home, in books, or in nature. Notice how the seedlings are alike and different. Draw the seedlings you see. Act out growing from a seed to a seedling.

Name: _____

The roots of plants take in water.

seed

seedling

root

Directions: Read about roots. Look at the pictures of a seed, seedling, and root. Draw lines from the words to the matching pictures.

Name: _____

A stem holds up leaves and flowers. Water and food move through the stem.

Plants

Directions: Read about stems. Color the examples of stems. Find stems in your home, books, or in nature. Notice how the stems are alike and different.

Name: _____

Leaves soak up sunlight. Plants need sunlight to live.

Time to Draw

Directions: Read about leaves. Color the examples of leaves. Draw a different type of leaf.

Plants

Name: _____

A flower is the blossom of a plant.

Time to Draw

Directions: Read about flowers. Color the examples of flowers. Find flowers in your home, in books, or in nature. Notice how the flowers are alike and different. Draw one of the flowers you see. Dance as if you are a flower.

130221—180 Days of Science

A fruit grows from a flower. We can eat many kinds of fruit.

Time to Draw

Directions: Read about fruit. Color the examples of fruit. Find fruit in your home, in books, or in nature. Notice how the fruits are alike and different. Draw one of the fruits you see.

Name: _____

Plants can climb. The vines of some plants grow around things to reach for the sun.

vines

Time to Draw

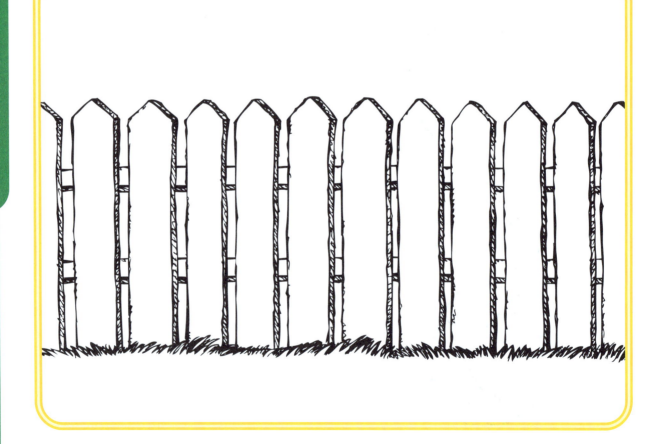

Directions: Read about plants that climb. Find plants that are climbers in your home, in books, or in nature. Notice how the plants climb on objects. Draw a plant climbing up the fence. Act out being a climbing plant.

Name: _____

Plants called  herbs can be used in cooking.

basil

rosemary

Directions: Read about herbs. Trace the word *herbs*. Color the examples of herbs. Find plants that are herbs in your home, in books, or in nature. Look and smell to see how the plants are similar and different.

Name: _____

A small sapling grows into a tree.

olive sapling   olive tree

Plants

Time to Draw

Directions: Read about trees. Color the examples of trees. Notice how the trees are similar and different. Draw a tree. Create and sing a song about trees.

Name: _____

Plants need water to live and grow. Plants take up water with their roots.

Are the plants watered?

Directions: Read about plants and water. Look at the examples of plants and water. Circle the pictures of plants that have been getting water. Color the pictures. Dance as if you are a plant that is getting water.

Name: _____

Plants need air to live and grow. Plants take in and give out air.

air

Time to Draw

Plants

Directions: Read about plants and air. Draw plants in the garden. Draw yourself watering the plants.

Name: _____

Plants need soil to live and grow.

Time to Draw

Directions: Read about plants and soil. Find plants in soil in your home, in books, or in your community. Draw the plants you see with their roots in the soil.

Name: _____

Plants need light to live and grow.

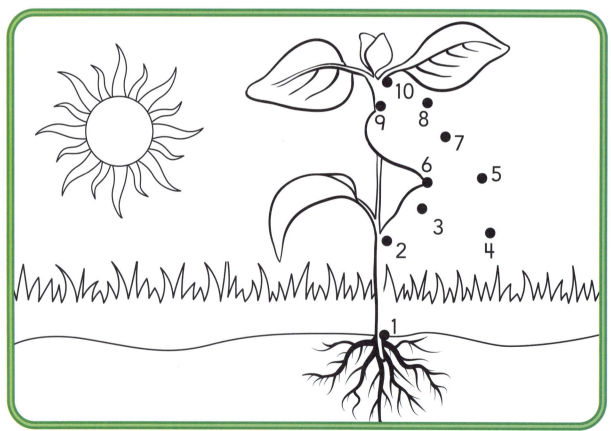

Directions: Read about plants and light. Trace the word *light*. Connect the dots, and color the picture.

Name: _____

Plants needs space to live and grow.

space →

Time to Draw

Directions: Read about plants and space. Look at the examples of plants with space to live and grow. Draw plants in the garden box with space to grow. Color your picture.

Animals

Name: _____

There are many different kinds of

animals.

Time to Draw

Directions: Read about animals. Trace the word *animals*. Color the examples of animals. Draw another animal you know. Act out being your favorite animal.

Name: _____

All animals need food to live and grow.

Animals

Which shows an animal eating food?

Which shows animals drinking water?

Directions: Read about animals and food. Circle the best answer to each question. Create a song about animals eating food.

Name: _____

Animals use their body parts to find and eat food.

f	o	o	d	i
j	f	o	o	d
g	c	b	a	z
e	f	o	o	d
f	o	o	d	l

Directions: Read about animals and food. Color the examples of animals eating food. Circle the word *food* four times in the word search. Act out different animals finding food.

Name: _____

All animals need

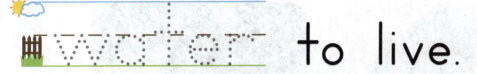

water to live.

Who is drinking?

Directions: Read about animals and water. Circle the pictures that show drinking water. Color the pictures. Act out being an animal that is drinking water.

Name: _____

Animals use their body parts to find and drink water.

 1

 2

 3

Directions: Read about animals and water. Look at the pictures. Draw lines to show the steps the giraffe takes to drink water.

Name: _____

All animals need to breathe. Some animals breathe air. Some breathe water.

Time to Draw

Directions: Read about animals breathing. Color the examples of animals breathing. Draw you and a friend breathing air outside. Color your picture. Tell a friend or adult about your picture.

Name: _____

Animals use their body parts to breathe.

nose

blowhole   **mouth**

Sharks breathe with their gills.

gills

Directions: Read about animals taking in air. Look at the pictures of animals breathing. Connect the dots to make the picture of a shark and its gills. Color the picture.

Animals

Name: _____

Animals use their

eyes to see.

dog

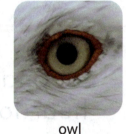
owl

iguana

chicken

Time to Draw

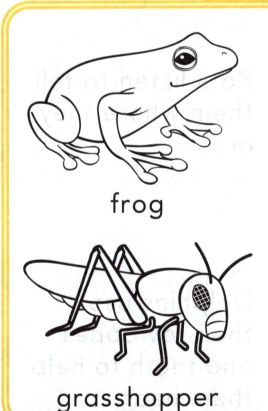
frog

grasshopper

Directions: Read about animal eyes. Trace the word *eyes*. Color the pictures. Find animal eyes in your home or in books. Draw the animal eyes you see. Create and sing a song about an animal with interesting eyes.

Name: _____

Animals hear with their ears.

cat

rat

cow

rabbit

Animals

Elephants can hear low sounds.

Bats listen to tell them where they are.

Dolphins use their jawbones and teeth to help them hear.

Directions: Read about animal ears. Look at the pictures of animal ears. Draw lines from the pictures to the matching sentences. Dance like an animal with interesting ears.

© Shell Education

Name: _____

Different animals have different body parts.

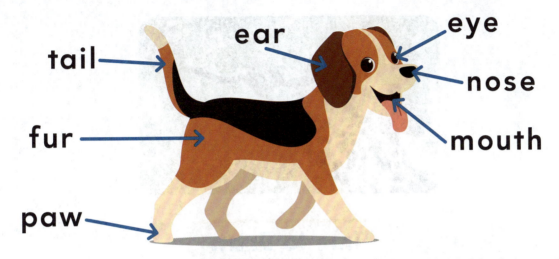

tail · ear · eye · nose · mouth · fur · paw

ear · eye · mane · nose · mouth · hoof · tail

Animals

Directions: Read about animal body parts. Look at the body parts of a dog. Read the names of the body parts of a horse. Draw lines from the words to the matching body parts. Talk about how the body parts of a dog and horse are alike and different.

Name: _____

Animals

Some animals have special body parts that help them live.

Time to Draw

Directions: Read about special body parts. Color the examples of animals with special body parts. Circle the special body parts. Draw an animal with special body parts.

Name: _____

To grasp means to hold onto an object. Animals use body parts to grasp.

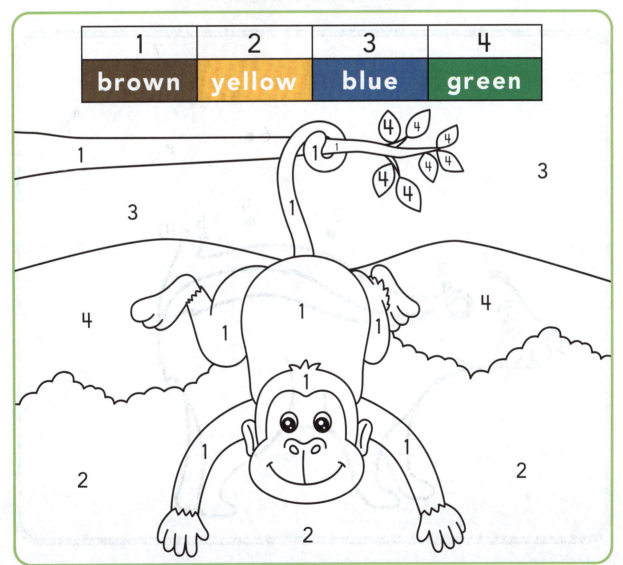

1	2	3	4
brown	**yellow**	**blue**	**green**

Directions: Read about animals grasping. Use the color key to complete the picture.

Name: _____

Animals use different parts of their bodies to protect themselves.

Animals

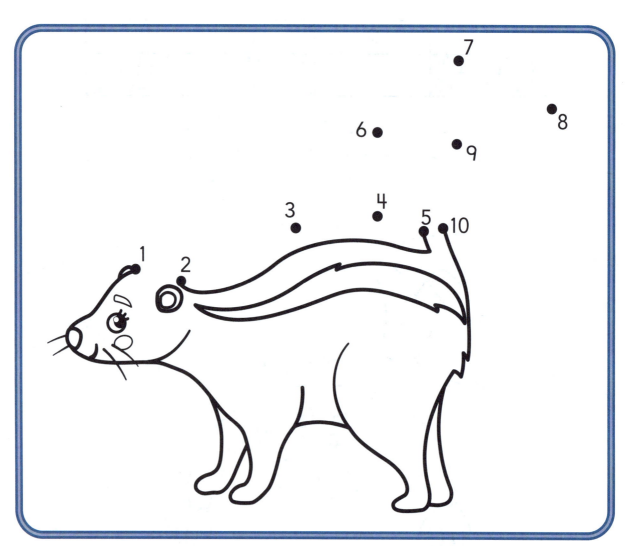

Directions: Read about animals protecting themselves. Connect the dots to make the picture of an animal protecting itself. Color the picture.

Name: _____

Animals move in different ways.

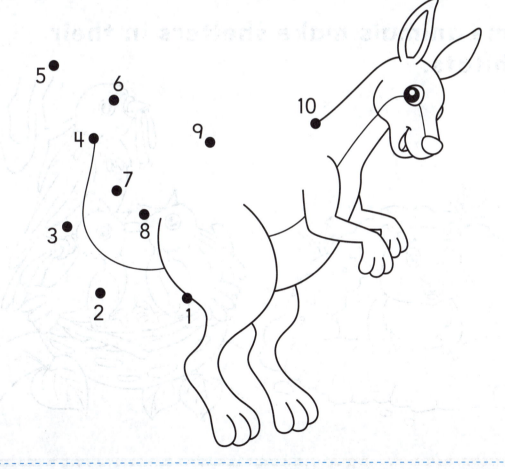

Directions: Read about animals moving. Trace the word *move*. Look at the pictures of how animals can move. Talk about how these animals move. Tell how they are alike and different. Connect the dots to make the picture of a kangaroo moving. Color the picture.

Animals

Name: _____

All animals have a natural place where they should live. That place is called a habitat.

Time to Color

Some animals make shelters in their habitats.

Directions: Read about animal habitats. Look at the pictures of animal habitats and shelters. Color the examples of animal shelters. Act out animals making or using shelters.

Name: _____

Succulents have thick leaves. They hold water for when the weather is dry. Young succulents look like parent plants.

Time to Draw

Directions: Read about young and parent succulents. Look at the pictures of young and parent succulents. Find succulents in books, your home, or the community. Draw a young and parent succulent. Color your picture.

Name: _____

Cactus plants have spines and thick stems. Young cactus plants look like parent plants.

Traits

spines

Directions: Read about young and parent cacti. Look at the pictures of cacti. Find cacti in books, your home, or your community. Connect the numbers from 1–10 to make a picture of a cactus. Color the picture.

Name: _____

Ferns have fronds. They do not have flowers. Young ferns look like parent plants.

frond

Time to Draw

Directions: Read about young and parent ferns. Look at the pictures of young and parent ferns. Find ferns in books, your home, or your community. Draw fronds on the young and parent fern pictures. Color the pictures.

Name: _____

Fig trees grow figs. Young and parent fig trees have leaves that are the same shape. Young fig trees look like parent plants.

Time to Draw

Directions: Read about young and parent fig trees. Look at the pictures of young and parent fig trees and figs. Draw figs on the tree. Color the picture.

Name: _____

Pine trees have narrow needles for leaves. They have cones. Young pine trees look like parent plants.

cones and needles

Time to Draw

Directions: Read about young and parent pine trees. Look at the pictures of young and parent trees, pine cones, and pine needles. Draw a pine tree with needles and cones. Color your picture.

Name: _____

A young kangaroo is called a joey. A joey lives in its mother's pouch when it is little. Joeys look like parent kangaroos.

Directions: Read about young and parent kangaroos. Look at the pictures. Circle the joeys in the picture. Color the picture. Jump like you are a kangaroo.

Name: _____

A young horse is called a foal. Foals look like parent horses.

Time to Draw

Directions: Read about young and parent horses. Look at the pictures. Find horses and foals in books or in your community. Draw a foal to go with the parent horse. Color the picture.

Traits

Name: _____

A young panda is called a cub. Panda cubs look like their parents.

Directions: Read about young and parent pandas. Look at the pictures. Use the examples of pandas to color the parent panda. Color the rest of the picture.

Name: _____

A young pig is called a piglet. Piglets look like parent pigs.

Directions: Read about young and parent pigs. Look at the pictures. Find pigs and piglets in books or in your community. Color the picture. Circle the piglets. Write the number of piglets in the picture.

Name: _____

A young giraffe is called a calf. Young calves look like parent giraffes.

Time to Color

Directions: Read about young and parent giraffes. Look at the pictures. Find giraffes and calves in books. Color the picture of the giraffes. Be sure to give them spots. Then, walk like a giraffe.

Name: _____

Living things are alive. People, animals, and plants are alive. Living things can grow and have babies.

Nonliving things are not alive. Nonliving things cannot grow or have babies.

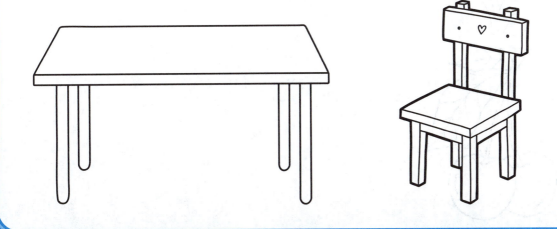

Directions: Read about living things. Color the examples of living things. Read about nonliving things. Color the examples of nonliving things. Find things around you. Say which things are living and which things are nonliving.

Living and Nonliving

Name: _____

A plant is a living thing. A plant has roots, a stem, and leaves. Plants may also have flowers and fruit.

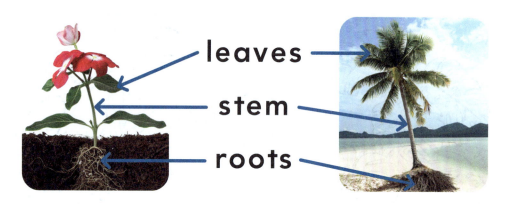

leaves

stem

roots

Time to Draw

I see flowers and fruit.

Directions: Read about plants. Look at the pictures of plant parts. Talk about different flowers and fruits you know. Color the pictures. Draw a flower and a fruit. Go on a scavenger hunt to find plants, and tell about their parts.

Name: _____

Mammals are living things. They have hair or fur.

1	2	3	4
black	orange	pink	tan

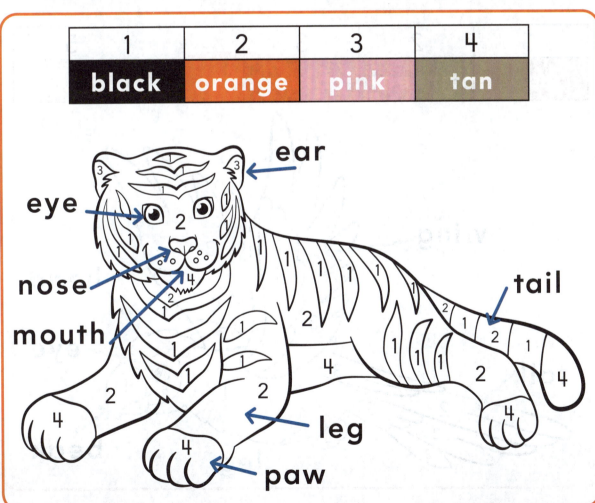

ear

eye

nose

mouth

tail

leg

paw

Directions: Read about mammals. Look at the pictures of mammals. Use the color key to complete the picture. Read the names of the tiger's body parts.

Name: _____

Birds are living things. They have feathers, wings, and beaks. Most birds can fly.

1	2	3	4	5
red	green	blue	yellow	pink

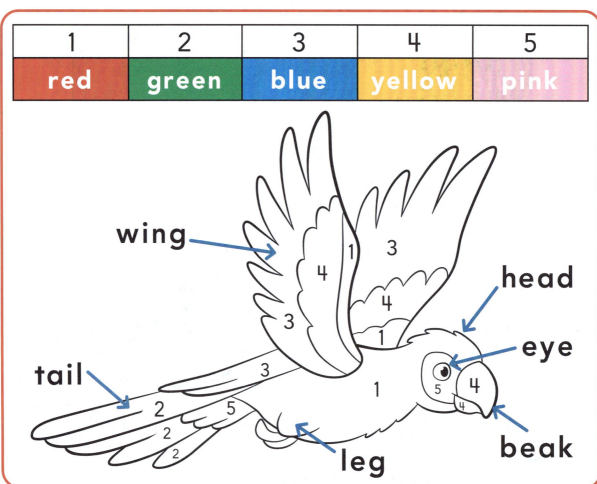

Directions: Read about birds. Look at the pictures of birds. Use the color key to complete the picture. Read the names of the body parts. Go on a scavenger hunt with an adult to find birds. Name the body parts you see.

Name: _____

Fish are living things. They live in water. They have fins for swimming. They have scales on their skin.

1	2	3	4	5
orange	green	blue	yellow	pink

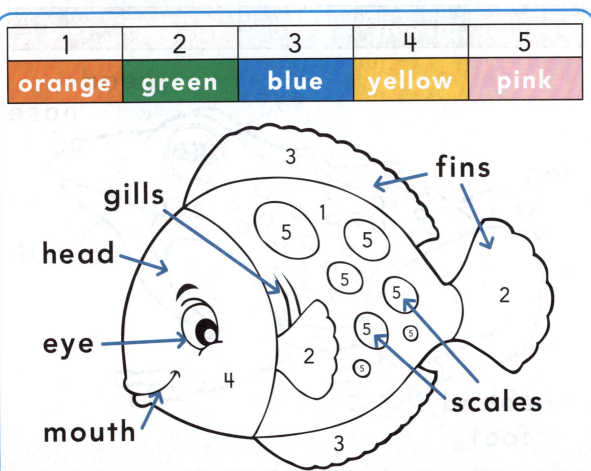

Directions: Read about fish. Look at the pictures of fish. Use the color key to complete the picture. Read the names of the body parts. Move like you are a fish using your fins.

Living and Nonliving

Name: _____

Amphibians are living things. They have smooth, slimy skin and webbed feet.

frog

newt

salamander

1	2	3	4	5
orange	green	blue	yellow	red

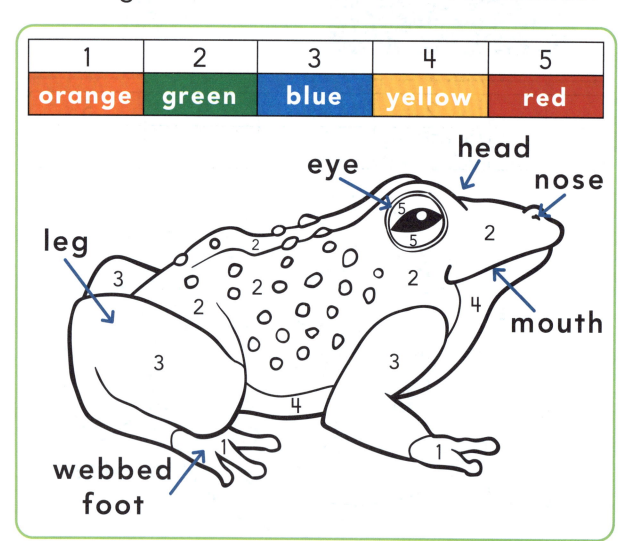

Directions: Read about amphibians. Look at the pictures of amphibians. Use the color key to complete the picture. Read the names of the body parts. Pretend you are a toad, and hop across the room.

Name: _____

Reptiles are living things. Reptiles have dry skin covered with scales.

snake

turtle

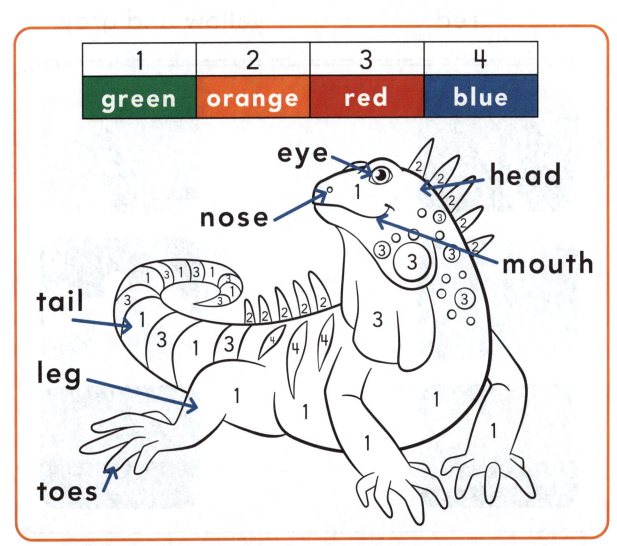

1	2	3	4
green	orange	red	blue

eye nose head mouth tail leg toes

Directions: Read about reptiles. Look at the pictures of reptiles. Use the color key to complete the picture. Read the names of the body parts. Crawl like a reptile with four legs. Slither like a snake.

Living and Nonliving

Name: _____

We can sort plants and animals by color. This tree and frog are both red. This flower and squirrel are not the same color.

red   yellow and gray

Directions: Read about sorting plants and animals. Find colorful plants and animals in books, your home, or your community. Talk about the colors of these living things. Draw lines to show how to sort the plants and animals by color.

Name: _____

We can sort plants and animals by size. This tree and elephant are both large. This seedling and mouse are both small.

large   small

Living and Nonliving

Directions: Read about sorting plants and animals. Find large and small plants and animals in books, your home, or your community. Talk about the sizes of these living things. Draw lines to show how to sort the plants and animals by size.

Name: _____

We can sort animals by how their bodies are covered. Animals have feathers, fur, scales, skin, or shells.

feathers   shells

fur

scales

skin

Living and Nonliving

Directions: Read about body coverings. Look at the pictures. Find different animal body coverings in books, your home, or your community. Talk about the body coverings. Draw lines to show how to sort the animals by body covering.

Name: _____

A seed is the part of a plant that can grow a new plant. A seedling is a young plant grown from a seed.

seeds

seedlings

Time to Draw

Life Cycle of a Plant

Directions: Read about seeds and seedlings. Look at the pictures of seeds and seedlings. Color the pumpkin seed and pumpkin seedling pictures. Draw a seed and seedling. Color the picture. Act out being a seed growing into a seedling.

Name: _____

A plant is a living thing. Most plants have leaves, stems, roots, and flowers or cones.

Life Cycle of a Plant

Plants or Seeds?

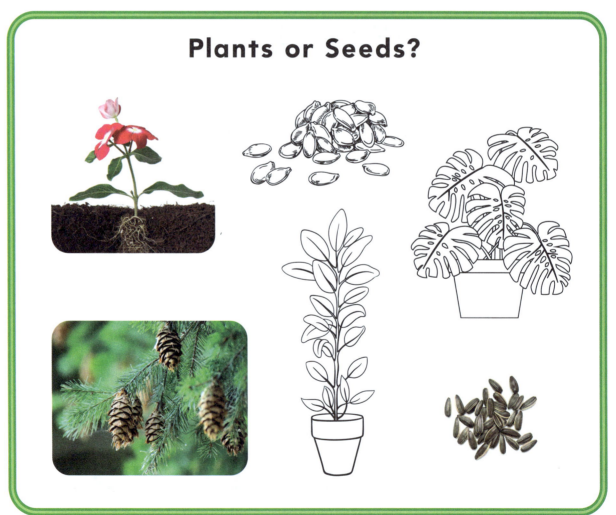

Directions: Read about plants. Circle each picture of a plant. Put an X next to each picture of seeds. Color the pictures. Dance as if you are a growing plant.

© Shell Education

Name: _____

A flower is the blossom of a plant. A fruit is the part of a plant that grows from a flower.

flowers

fruits

Flowers or Fruits?

Directions: Read about flowers and fruits. Look at the pictures of flowers and fruits. Circle each picture of a flower. Put an *X* next to each picture of a fruit. Color the pictures. Go on a scavenger hunt to find flowers and fruit.

Name: _____

Living things go through life cycles. Living things change as they grow. Plants have life cycles. Plants change as they grow.

Life Cycle of a Plant

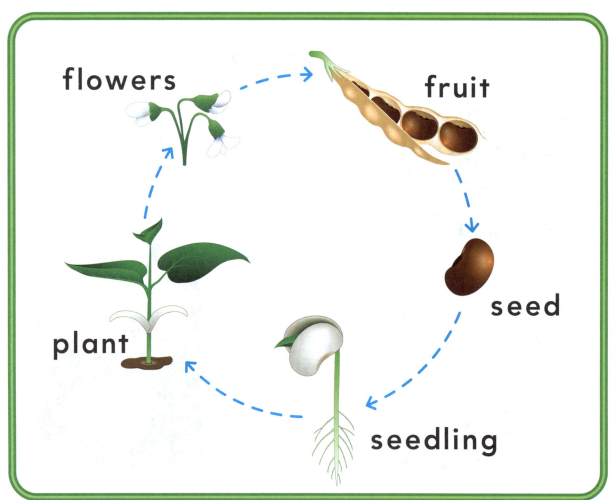

flowers

fruit

seed

seedling

plant

Directions: Read about life cycles. Look at the examples of how plants change over time. Trace the arrows on the bean plant life cycle. Talk about the life cycle of a bean plant. Act out the life cycle of a plant.

Name: _____

I see the life cycle of an apple tree.

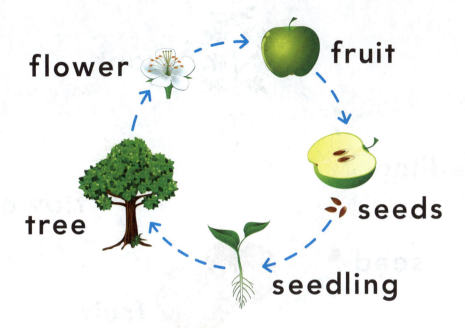

flower

fruit

seeds

seedling

tree

Time to Draw

Directions: Look at the life cycle of an apple tree. Trace the arrows on the life cycle. Draw your favorite part of an apple tree's life cycle.

Name: _____

Life Cycle of a Plant

I see the life cycle of a tomato plant.

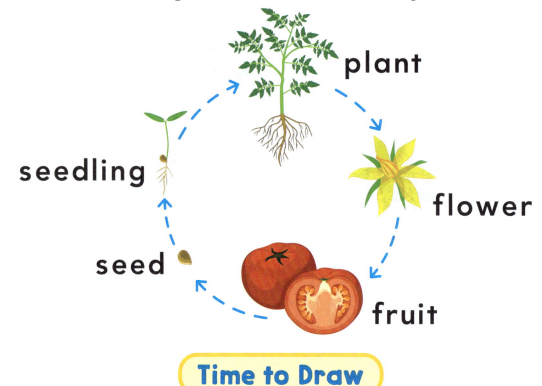

plant

flower

fruit

seed

seedling

Time to Draw

Directions: Look at the life cycle of a tomato plant. Trace the arrows on the life cycle. Draw your favorite part of a tomato plant's life cycle. Act out planting tomato seeds.

Name: _____

I see the life cycle of a strawberry plant.

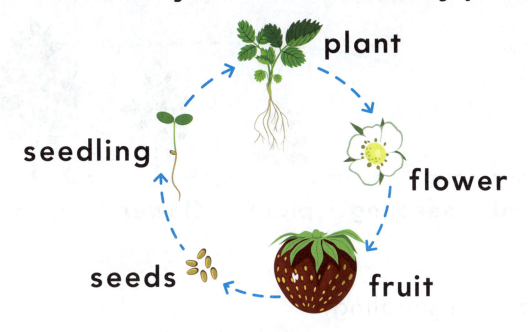

Time to Draw

Directions: Look at the life cycle of a strawberry plant. Trace the arrows on the life cycle. Look at the life cycle of an orange tree. Talk about what is happening in the picture. Draw the fruit that is shown in this life cycle.

Name: _____

I see the life cycle of a lemon tree.

Life Cycle of a Plant

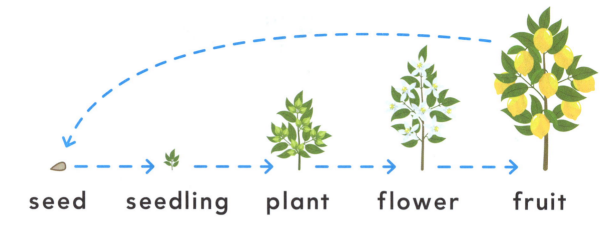

seed   seedling   plant   flower   fruit

Which is a seedling?

Which is a lemon seed?

Directions: Look at the life cycle of a lemon tree. Trace the arrows on the life cycle. Talk about the life cycle of a lemon tree. Circle the correct answers to the questions.

Name: _____

I see the life cycle of a chili pepper plant.

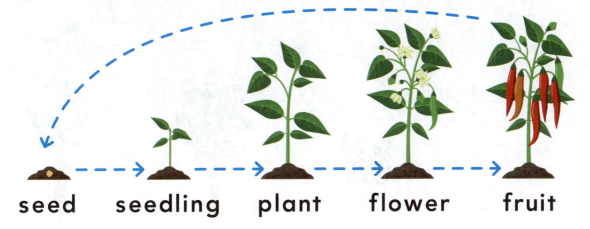

seed   seedling   plant   flower   fruit

Time to Draw

Directions: Look at the life cycle of a chili pepper plant. Trace the arrows on the life cycle. Draw chili pepper flowers on one plant. Draw peppers on the other plant. Color the pictures. Dance as if you have eaten a spicy chili pepper.

Name: _____

I see the life cycle of a carrot plant.

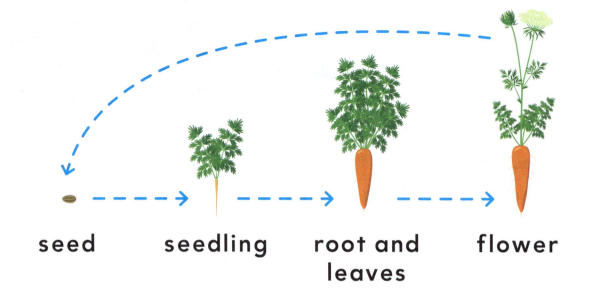

seed   seedling   root and   flower
                                leaves

How a Carrot Grows

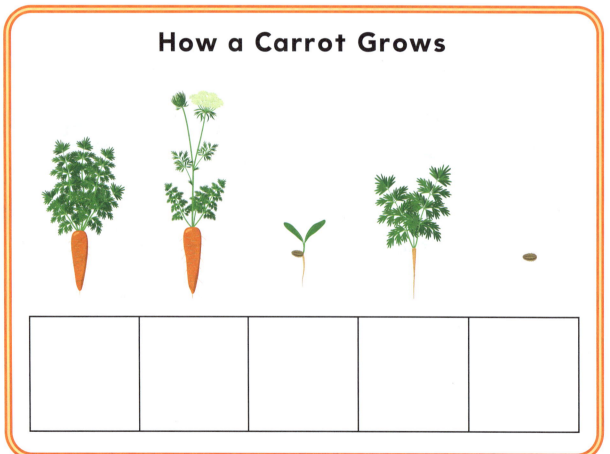

Directions: Look at the life cycle of a carrot plant. Trace the arrows on the life cycle. Look at the pictures of a carrot growing. Write the numbers *1, 2, 3, 4,* and *5* to show the correct order of the pictures.

Name: _____

Motion is when an object moves. To push means to press or move away an object.

Time to Draw

I can push.

Directions: Read the text. Look at the examples of pushes. Color the examples. Push a few objects around you, and notice what happens. Draw objects you can push.

Pushes and Pulls

Name: _____

To push means to press or move away an object.

Pushes and Pulls

Air blows bubbles.

Water pushes ducks.

Directions: Read about pushing. Color the examples of pushing without touching. Find things you can use to experiment with. Practice pushing them with air or water. Talk about what you see.

Name: _____

To pull means to drag or tug an object toward you.

push

pull

Directions: Read about pulling. Draw lines from the words to match the pictures of pushing and pulling.

Name: _____

To pull means to drag or tug an object toward you.

Pushes and Pulls

Time to Draw

Directions: Read about pulling. Look at the example of pulling. Find items you can use to experiment with. Use these objects to practice pulling. Talk about what you see. Draw yourself pulling an object.

We can push and pull.

Directions: Read the sentence. Talk about the examples of pushing and pulling. Circle the pictures of pushes. Write *X*s over the pictures of pulls. Act out moving objects with pushes and pulls.

Pushes and Pulls

Name: _____

Strength means to use power or force.

Time to Draw

I can push and pull with much strength.

Directions: Read about strength. Color the examples of pushing and pulling with much strength. Find items you may use to experiment with. Use these objects to practice pushing and pulling with much strength. Draw what you can push and pull with much strength.

Strength means to use power or force.

Time to Draw

I can push and pull with less strength.

Directions: Read about strength. Color the examples of pushing and pulling with less strength. Find items you may use to experiment with. Use these objects to practice pushing and pulling with less strength. Draw what you can push and pull with less strength.

Name: _____

Pushes and Pulls

Direction is the path that something moves in or points to.

Time to Draw

I can change the direction of an object.

up   down

Directions: Read about direction. Look at the example showing direction. Color the picture of changing direction. Find things to practice moving up and down. Use these objects to practice pushing and pulling up and down. Draw your experiments.

Direction is the path that something moves in or points to.

Time to Draw

I can change the direction of an object.

left

right

Directions: Read about direction. Look at the example showing direction. Color the pictures of changing direction. Find things to practice moving left and right. Use these objects to practice pushing and pulling left and right. Draw your experiments.

Name: _____

I can build a toy to put in motion.

Time to Draw

My Plan

Directions: Read the text. Trace the word *motion.* Look at the examples of toys that move. Draw a plan to build a toy you can push or pull to put in motion. Find things to build this toy. Build the toy. Talk about how your toy can move.

Pushes and Pulls

Name: _____

Speed is how fast an object moves.

Time to Draw

Objects can move at different speeds.

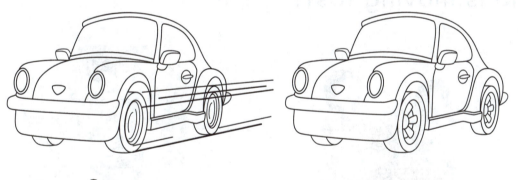

fast   slow

Directions: Read about speed. Look at the example showing speed. Color the pictures of changing speed. Find things to move fast and slow. Use these objects to practice pushing at different speeds. Draw objects that move at fast and slow speeds.

Name: _____

Speed is how fast an object moves.

Who is moving fast?

Who is moving slowly?

Directions: Read about speed. Circle the best answer to each question.

Interactions

To start is to begin to move. We can push objects to start them moving.

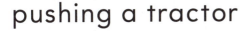

pushing a boat

pushing a tractor

pushing a car

Interactions

Directions: Read about pushing to start motion. Draw lines to match the phrases with the pictures. Talk about which of the objects in the pictures might keep moving after it is pushed. Pretend you are pushing a big rock to start it rolling down a hill.

Name: _____

To start is to begin to move. We can pull objects to start them moving.

Pushing or Pulling?

Interactions

Directions: Read about pulling to start motion. Talk about things that you pull to start. Circle the pictures of pulling to start motion. Pretend you are pulling something very heavy.

Name: _____

To stop means to keep something from moving.

We can push to stop motion.

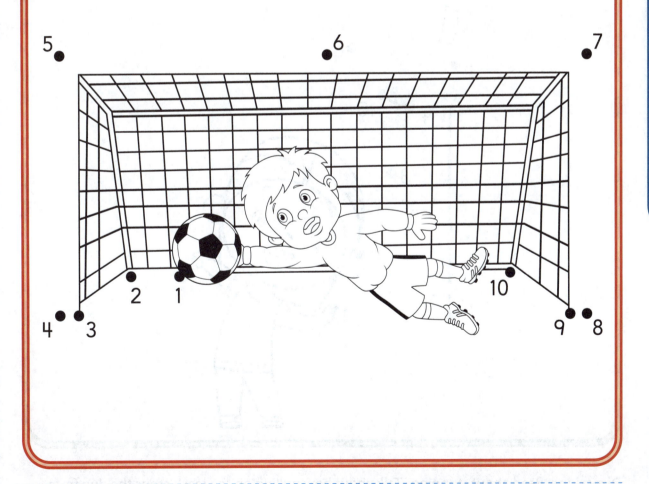

Directions: Read about stopping motion. Connect the dots to make the picture of stopping by pushing. Color the picture.

Name: _____

To stop means to keep something from moving. We can pull to stop motion.

Interactions

Directions: Read about stopping. Talk about how pulling on the leash stops the dog from moving in the picture. Connect the dots, and color the picture. Pretend you are pulling 100 balloons down to keep them from flying away.

Name: _____

When objects collide, they hit with strength.

Time to Draw

Toys can collide to stop.

Directions: Read about objects that collide. Look at the example of objects colliding. Find things to practice colliding. Draw your experiments.

Name: _____

When objects collide, they hit with strength. Objects that collide can change motion.

Directions: Read about objects that collide. Look at the examples of objects colliding to change motion. Draw lines to show the steps for marbles colliding and changing motion.

Name: _____

A 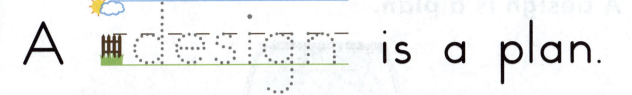 is a plan.

start

stop

Energy and Forces

fast

slow

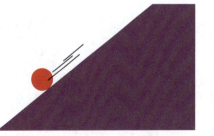

Directions: Read about a design. Trace the word *design*. Look at the design for a marble ramp. Draw a path for the marble on the design. Draw lines to match the ramps to the correct words.

Energy and Forces

Name: _____

A design is a plan.

Time to Draw

My Pinball Game Design

Directions: Read about a design. Look at the pinball machine design. Find things you can use to make your own pinball game. Draw your pinball game design. Use the objects to make your design.

Name: _____

We can push to put an object in motion.

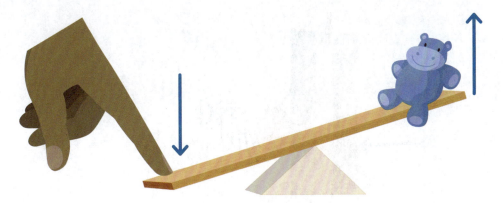

Time to Draw

My Design

Directions: Read about objects in motion. Look at the example of pushing to make something move. Find things you can use to experiment with. Draw your own design for pushing to make something move. Build your design, and practice with it.

Name: _____

We can push to put an object in motion.

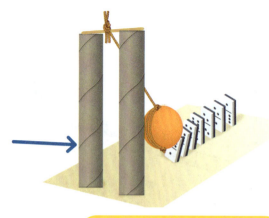

Time to Draw

My Design

Energy and Forces

Directions: Read about objects in motion. Look at the example of moving an object by pushing. Find things you may use to experiment with. Draw your own design for moving an object by pushing. Build your design, and practice with it.

Name: _____

We can pull to put an object in motion.

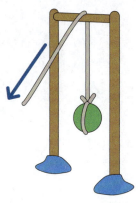

Time to Draw

My Design

Directions: Read about objects in motion. Look at the picture of moving an object by pulling. Find things you can use to experiment with. Draw your own design for moving an object by pulling. Build your design, and practice with it.

Name: _____

We can pull to put an object in motion.

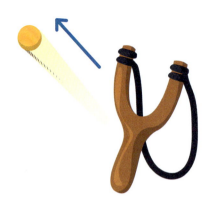

Time to Draw

My Design

Directions: Read about objects in motion. Look at the example of moving an object by pulling. Find things you can use to experiment with. Draw your own design for moving an object by pulling. Build your design, and practice with it.

Energy and Forces

Name: _____

We can pull to put an object in motion.

Time to Draw

My Design

Directions: Read about objects in motion. Look at the example of moving an object by pulling. Find things you can use to experiment with. Draw your own design for moving an object by pulling. Build your design, and practice with it.

Name: _____

Energy and Forces

Objects can move at different speeds. They can move fast and slow.

Time to Draw

My Design

Directions: Read about objects moving at different speeds. Look at the examples of ramps. Talk about how objects can roll down them at different speeds. Find things you can use to make ramps. Test to see how fast objects roll down the ramps. Draw your experiments.

Name: _____

We can start an object in motion.

Time to Draw

My Design

Directions: Read about starting objects in motion. Look at the example of starting an object in motion. Find things you can use to experiment with. Draw your own design to start an object in motion. Build your design, and practice with it.

Name: _____

We can stop an object in motion.

Energy and Forces

Time to Draw

My Design

Directions: Read about stopping objects in motion. Look at the example of stopping an object in motion. Find things you can use to experiment with. Draw your own design to stop an object in motion. Build your design, and practice with it.

Name: _____

Objects stop or change motion when they collide. To collide means to hit together.

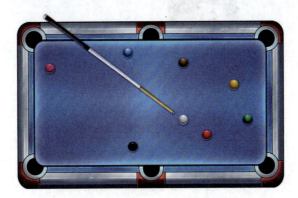

Time to Draw

My Design

Directions: Read about objects that collide. Look at the example of colliding to stop or change direction. Find things you can use to experiment with. Draw your own design for a game where marbles collide. Build your design, and practice with it.

Name: _____

Objects can collide with strength.

Time to Draw

My Design

Directions: Read about objects that collide. Look at the example of objects colliding. Find things you can use to experiment with. Draw your own design for a game where objects collide. Build your design, and practice with it.

Name: _____

Land is the solid part of Earth. Sunlight shines on the land.

land

Time to Draw

Directions: Read about the sunlight and land. Look at the pictures of sunlight shining on land. See what the land in your community looks like when the sunlight shines on it. Draw what you see.

Name: _____

Some kinds of land are sand, soil, and rock.

sand

soil

rock

Directions: Read about the kinds of land. Trace the word *land*. Talk about the kinds of land in your community. Draw lines to match the kinds of land with the pictures. Act out walking across rocky land.

Sunlight warms the land on Earth's surface.

sand

soil

rocks

Directions: Read about sunlight warming the land. Color the pictures of sand, soil, and rocks. Take a walk with an adult to natural land near you to feel the warmth of the sun there.

Name: _____

Water is the liquid part of Earth. Sunlight affects the water on Earth's surface.

water

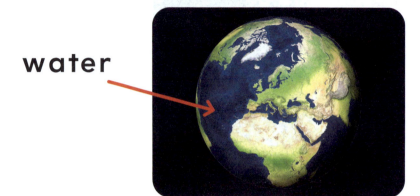

Directions: Read about sunlight and water. Color the pictures of the sun shining on water. Talk about the water in your community. Dance as if you are water.

Some kinds of water are oceans, lakes, and rivers.

ocean

lake

river

Directions: Read about kinds of water on Earth. Circle the pictures of oceans. Create and sing a song about kinds of water.

Name: _____

Sunlight **warms the water on Earth.**

Sunlight's Effect on Earth

ocean

river

lake

Time to Draw

Directions: Read about sunlight and water. Trace the word *warms*. Look at the pictures of sunlight warming water. Draw the sun warming a lake. Add boats and people having fun.

© Shell Education

Name: _____

Sunlight warms the air. Sunlight can warm places that are warm or cold.

Time to Draw

Directions: Read about sunlight warming the air. Look at the pictures of sunlight warming the air. Draw the sunlight warming the air in your community.

Name: _____

When the sun warms the air, it can make hot weather.

Directions: Read about how the sun warms the air. Talk about the pictures. Circle the pictures of warm days.

Name: _____

Sunlight warms the air. This makes the weather change.

rain

snow

sun

sun

rain

snow

Directions: Read about how the sun changes the weather. Draw lines from the words to match the pictures.

Name: _____

Plants grow in the sunlight. Many animals and people eat plants.

Sunlight's Effect on Earth

Time to Draw

I eat plants.

Directions: Read about sunlight and plants. Look at the examples of plants that people eat. Draw plants that you like to eat. Dance like an animal eating plants.

Name: _____

Shade is darkness when the sun is blocked. Shade shelters us from the sun.

Time to Draw

I see shade.

Directions: Read about shade. Look at the examples of shade. Find how shade looks in your community. Draw a shaded area you see. Create and sing a song about finding shade outside your home.

Name: _____

A design is a plan for something. You can design something that makes shade and protects you from sunlight.

Time to Draw

My Design

Directions: Read about making a design. Look at the designs for making shade. Design something that makes shade for a yard. Draw your design. Work with an adult to build a model of your design. Try out your model to see if it makes shade.

Name: _____

Sometimes, we need shade in a car. You can design a shade for a car.

Time to Draw

My Design

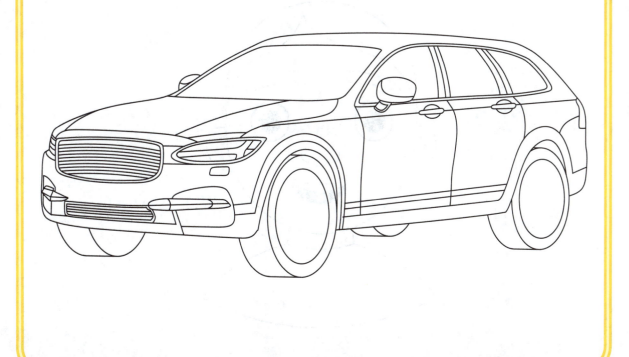

Directions: Read about making shade in a car. Look at the examples of shades in cars. Circle the example you think works best. Draw a way to make shade in the car. Color the picture.

Name: _____

Reducing Warming Effect of Sunlight

Sunglasses protect our eyes from the sun. You can design sunglasses to shade your eyes.

Time to Draw

My Design

Directions: Read about sunglasses. Look at the examples of sunglasses. Draw a design for sunglasses. Color your design. Pretend that you are walking in the sun with your sunglasses on.

Name: _____

Sometimes, we need to shade our bodies from the sun. This is personal shade. You can design personal shade.

Time to Draw

My Design

Directions: Read about personal shade. Look at the examples of personal shade. Draw two designs for personal shade. Talk about how your designs will protect you from the sunlight.

Reducing Warming Effect of Sunlight

Name: _____

Gardens need shade from the sunlight. Many plants in a garden live and grow in the shade.

Time to Draw

My Design

Directions: Read about shade in gardens. Look at the examples of shade in gardens. Design some shade for a garden. Draw and color your design. Talk about your garden shade design.

Name: _____

A playground should have some shade from the sun.

s	h	a	d	e	b
d	s	h	a	d	e
e	k	o	o	d	i
f	s	h	a	d	e
s	h	a	d	e	d

Directions: Read about playground shade. Look at the examples of playground shade. Talk about how shade looks at a playground in your community. Find and circle the word *shade* four times in the word search.

Reducing Warming Effect of Sunlight

Name: _____

I can design shade for a playground.

Time to Draw

My Design

Directions: Read the sentence. Talk with an adult to design shade for a playground. Draw your design. Use tools and materials to build a model of your design.

People need shade from the sun at the beach.

Shade at the Beach

Directions: Read about shade at the beach. Look at the examples of shade at the beach. Find how shade looks at the beach in books or near your community. Circle the pictures that show shade at the beach.

Name: _____

I can design a shade for the beach.

Reducing Warming Effect of Sunlight

Time to Draw

My Design

Directions: Read the sentence. Look at the example of shade at the beach. Draw a design for a shade at the beach. Draw the sun in your picture. Color your picture.

Name: _____

Weather changes. It can be hot or cold. It can be rainy, snowy, or dry. We can see and feel the weather.

Time to Draw

I see _weather_.

Directions: Read about weather. Trace the word *weather*. Draw different types of weather you have seen. Dance like different types of weather.

Name: _____

Sunlight is the light of the sun. The sun warms Earth.

Sunlight shines during the day.

Directions: Read about sunlight. Circle the examples of sunlight. Draw the sun.

Name: _____

 Wind is moving air.

Time to Draw

I can see wind blowing.

Directions: Read about wind. Trace the word *wind*. Draw wind blowing. Dance like the wind.

Name: _____

Weather and Climate

Snow is made of tiny crystals of ice that fall from clouds.

When it snows, the temperature is cold.

Directions: Read about snow. Circle the pictures of snow in cold temperatures. Create and sing a song about snow.

Name: _____

Rain is water that falls from clouds in drops.

Weather and Climate

Time to Draw

1. Draw raindrops.

2. Draw a rain puddle.

3. Draw an umbrella.

Directions: Read about rain. Look at the examples of rain. Follow the steps to draw a picture about rain. Act out being in the rain.

Weather and Climate

Name: _____

We see a rainbow when light shines through water droplets. Rainbows may form when it rains.

Time to Color

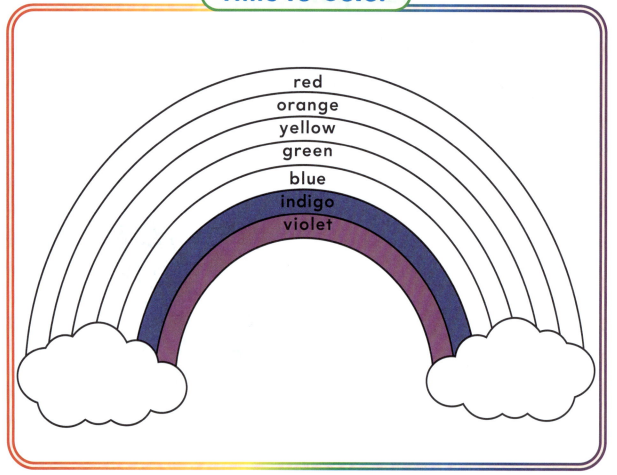

red
orange
yellow
green
blue
indigo
violet

Directions: Read about rainbows. Look at the example of a rainbow. Talk about the colors in a rainbow. Color the rainbow.

Name: _____

Clouds are made from tiny water drops and ice crystals. They float together in the air.

Time to Draw

Four Main Types of Clouds

cumulus   cirrus   nimbus   stratus

Directions: Read about clouds. Look at the examples of clouds. Find clouds in books or in your community. Draw pictures of different types of clouds.

Name: _____

The temperature is how warm or cold the air is.

Time to Draw

hot and sunny	cold and snowy

Directions: Read about temperature. Draw a hot, sunny day and a cold, snowy day. Talk about what you enjoy doing in hot and cold temperatures.

Name: _____

Weather has patterns. The weather may be cool in the morning and warm in the afternoon. That is a weather pattern.

Time to Draw

Directions: Read about weather patterns. Talk about the weather pattern at the beach in the pictures. Draw a picture showing you in the kind of weather you like best.

Name: _____

Climate is what the weather is like in a place most of the time. The climate of a desert is dry. The climate of a rain forest is wet.

wet climate

freezing climate

dry climate

Directions: Read about climate. Look at the examples of places with different climates. Talk about the climate in your community. Draw lines to match the climates with the correct pictures.

Name: _____

The environment is all the natural things around us. Trees can change the environment.

Time to Draw

Directions: Read about trees. Look at the examples of how trees can change the environment. Color the examples of how trees can change the environment. Draw a tree that is changing the environment.

Name: _____

Plant roots can change the environment.

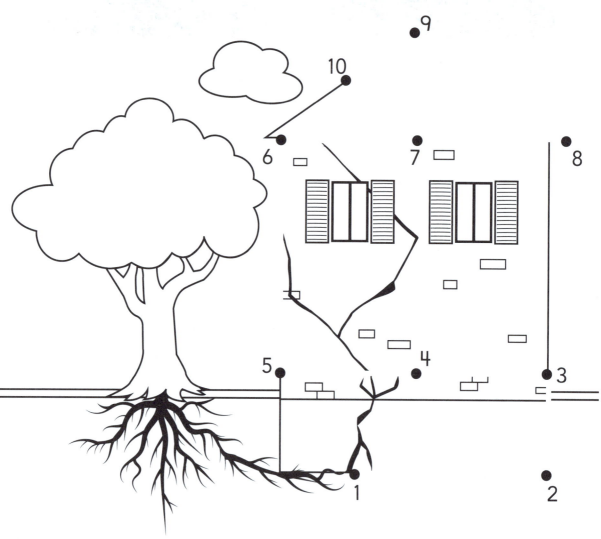

Directions: Read about plants and roots. Look at the examples of roots changing the environment. Find roots that change the environment in books or in your community. Connect the dots to complete the picture. Color the picture.

Name: _____

Forests can change the environment. Forests help make clean air. Forests are home to animals.

Time to Draw

Directions: Read about forests. Look at the examples of animals that live in forests. Draw an animal living in the forest. Act out animals living in forests.

Name: _____

Seeds change the environment. They grow into plants.

Time to Draw

Directions: Read about seeds. Look at the examples of plants that make seeds. Look at the picture of how seeds can change the environment by growing new apple trees. Draw a seed growing into a plant.

Name: _____

Gardens change the environment.

Time to Color

Directions: Read about gardens. Look at the examples of gardens. Find gardens that change the environment in books or in your community. Color the picture. Talk about how this garden is changing the environment.

Name: _____

Beavers change the environment. They build dams to live in.

Changing Environments

1

2

3

Directions: Read about beavers. Look at the picture of a beaver dam. Talk about how beavers change the environment. Match the numbers to the pictures to show how the beaver builds a dam. Color the pictures.

Name: _____

Rabbits change the environment. They eat plants and build nests.

Changing Environments

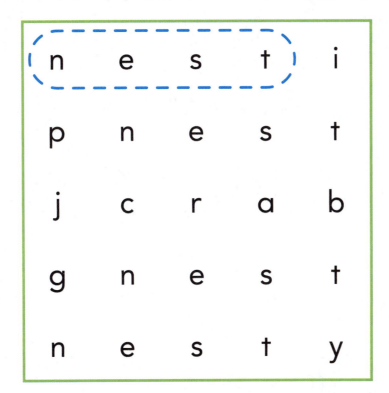

```
n  e  s  t  i

p  n  e  s  t

j  c  r  a  b

g  n  e  s  t

n  e  s  t  y
```

Directions: Read about rabbits. Color the pictures of rabbits changing the environment. Find and circle the word *nest* four times in the word search. Act out being a rabbit eating plants.

Name: _____

Dogs can change the environment. They can dig holes. Parks are made for them to play in.

Time to Draw

Directions: Read about dogs. Look at the pictures of dogs changing the environment. Find dogs that change the environment in books or in your community. Draw dogs that change the environment.

© Shell Education

Changing Environments

Name: _____

Woodpeckers change the environment. They look for bugs in trees. They use their beaks to make holes in the trees.

Time to Draw

Directions: Read about woodpeckers. Look at the pictures of woodpeckers changing the environment. Draw holes made by the woodpeckers on the trees. Color the picture. Talk about how woodpeckers change trees.

Name: _____

Prairie dogs change the environment. They burrow underground. They eat plants and move dirt around.

Time to Color

Directions: Read about prairie dogs. Look at the pictures of prairie dogs changing the environment. Color the picture of prairie dog tunnels. Act out being a prairie dog making a tunnel.

Name: _____

Humans change the environment by digging. Digging for metals and gems is called mining.

Time to Color

Directions: Read about humans changing the environment. Look at the pictures of mining. Color the pictures of mining tools. Act out mining.

Name: _____

Humans change the environment by cutting down trees. This is called logging. New trees are sometimes planted.

Directions: Read about logging. Look at the pictures of how logging changes the environment. Circle the pictures of people planting trees to regrow the forest.

Name: _____

We can help protect nature from human change.

Time to Draw

Directions: Read about protecting nature. Look at the pictures of protected natural places. Find protected natural places in books or in your community. Draw a natural place that is special to you. Create and sing a song about ways to protect nature.

Name: _____

We can protect

animals and wildlife.

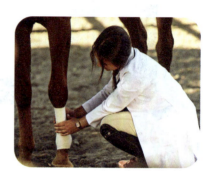

Time to Draw

Directions: Read about protecting animals. Trace the word *animals*. Look at the pictures of humans protecting animals. Draw humans helping animals. Talk about how protecting animals changes the environment.

Name: _____

Humans make the air, water, and land dirty. This is called polluting. This changes the environment.

Time to Color

Directions: Read about polluting. Look at the pictures of pollution. Color the picture. Help the family clean up by circling 5 pieces of trash. Act out cleaning up trash.

Name: _____

Farming changes the environment. Farmers grow plants or raise animals.

Time to Draw

Directions: Read about farming. Find farms in books or in your community. Draw a farmer growing plants on the land. Color the picture.

Name: _____

Buildings change the environment. We use things such as wood, rocks, and steel to build.

Time to Draw

Directions: Read about buildings changing the environment. Look at the pictures of buildings. Find buildings in your community. Draw the buildings you see. Talk about how these buildings have changed the land.

Name: _____

Grass needs sunlight. It grows on open land where the sun can shine on it.

Directions: Read about grass. Look at the pictures of grass growing in the open. Find grass in books, at your home, or in your community. Circle the pictures of grass growing in the open. Create and sing a song about grass growing in the sunshine.

Name: _____

Bromeliads are a kind of plant. They grow in the rainforest. They need to catch water.

water

Time to Draw

Directions: Read about bromeliads. Notice how the plants catch water like cups. Draw a bromeliad plant. Color your picture. Act out being a bromeliad catching water.

Name: _____

Redwood trees grow in forests. The trees have thick bark that helps protect them from burning in fires.

redwood bark

fire

redwood tree

Directions: Read about redwood trees. Look at the examples of redwood trees and bark. Find trees in books, your neighborhood, or your community. Notice the different types of tree bark. Draw lines from the words to match the pictures.

Name: _____

Palm trees live in hot places. They have a thin layer of wax around the leaves to keep them from drying out.

Time to Draw

Directions: Read about palm trees. Look at the pictures of palm trees and their leaves. Find palm trees in books or your community. Notice the different kinds of leaves on the palm trees. Draw a tall palm tree.

Name: _____

Deer eat buds, fruit, moss, bark, and leaves. Deer need to live in forests. Forests have all these kinds of food.

Time to Color

Directions: Read about deer. Color the picture of a deer eating in the forest. Find deer in books, your neighborhood, or your community. Notice what the deer eat. Dance as if you are deer finding and eating food.

Name: _____

Pandas eat bamboo. They live in bamboo forests. A lot of bamboo grows there.

Time to Draw

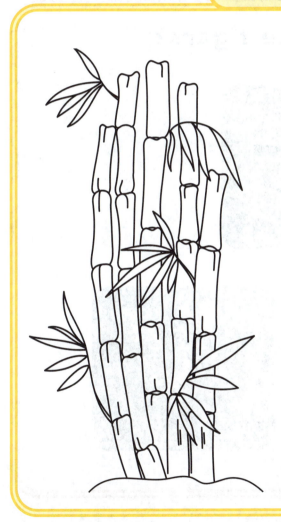

Directions: Read about pandas. Look at the pictures of pandas and bamboo. Color the bamboo green. Draw a panda eating bamboo. Act out being a panda eating bamboo.

Name: _____

Needs of Plants, Animals, and People

Tigers need to hunt for food. Their stripes help them hide from the animals they want to catch.

Where are the tigers?

Directions: Read about tigers. Look at the pictures of tigers. Talk about why tigers hide in nature. Find the tigers hiding in nature. Circle the hiding tigers. Act out being a tiger hiding in the shadows of trees and branches.

Name: _____

Humans travel in different ways depending on where they are. These people travel in the desert.

cars

camels

ATVs

camel

ATV

car

- -

Directions: Read about traveling in the desert. Look at the pictures of traveling in the desert. Talk about what people need to travel in the desert. Draw lines from the words to match the pictures. Color the pictures.

- -

Name: _____

Humans need to travel where they live. These people travel where it is very cold.

snowmobile

dogsled

truck

dogsled

truck

snowmobile

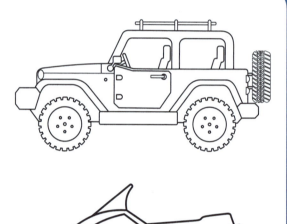

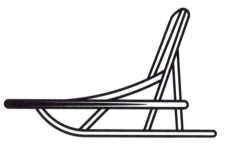

Directions: Read about travel on the frozen tundra. Look at the pictures of traveling where it is very cold. Draw lines from the words to match the pictures. Color the pictures. Pretend you are riding on a dogsled.

Needs of Plants, Animals, and People

Name: _____

Humans need to travel where they live. These people travel on the water that they live near.

rowboat

jet ski

ferry boat

Time to Draw

Directions: Read about travel on the water. Look at the pictures of traveling on the water. Draw a way to travel on the water. Pretend you are rowing a boat across the water.

Name: _____

Weather Forecasting

Humans live in different places. The weather in these places is different.

rain   snow   heat

People can predict what the weather will be like. This is called weather forecasting.

🟩 = rain

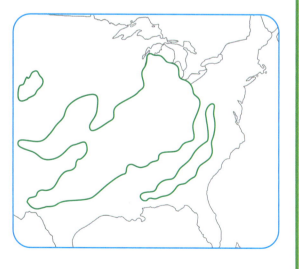

Directions: Read about weather and forecasting. Look at the pictures of weather. Talk about what the weather is like where you live. Look at the weather forecast. Talk about the green parts of the map that show rain. Color the parts of the forecast that show rain with green.

Name: _____

Forecasts show what the weather will be like for the day. Some show the weather for a week or more.

MON	TUE	WED	THU	FRI
74°	83°	75°	82°	81°
SUNNY	THUNDERSTORMS	MOSTLY CLOUDY	PARTLY CLOUDY	RAIN

Weather Forecasting

What will the temperature be on Monday?

81°

Which picture means partly cloudy?

How warm will Friday be?

74°

Which picture means thunderstorms?

Directions: Read about weather forecasts. Look at the forecast. Talk about what kinds of weather the forecast shows. Draw lines to match the questions with the correct pictures.

Weather Forecasting

Name: _____

The weather changes where you live. It is important to know what the weather will be like so you can be ready.

rain

snow

heat

Time to Draw

90°

SUNNY

Directions: Read about being ready for the weather. Look at the pictures of different weather. Talk about how you could be ready for the kinds of weather in the pictures. Talk about the weather forecast. Draw something you could wear to be ready for this weather.

Name: _____

Weather forecasting helps us get ready for the weather. Windy weather happens when the air moves very fast.

68°

WINDY

Directions: Read about windy weather. Look at the pictures of windy weather. Talk about how you could be ready for windy weather. Talk about the weather forecast. Circle the picture that shows windy weather.

Weather Forecasting

Name: _____

Dust storms happen when wind blows sand and dirt. Dust storms happen in the desert or where there is loose sand and dirt.

Time to Draw

Directions: Read about dust storms. Draw a dust storm. Talk about how people might stay safe during dust storms.

Name: _____

Thunderstorms often bring heavy rain. This can cause flooding.

thunderstorm   heavy rain   flooding

Time to Draw

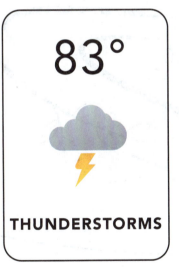

83°

THUNDERSTORMS

Directions: Read about thunderstorms and floods. Look at the pictures of thunderstorms and flooding. Talk about thunder and lightning you have seen and heard. Talk about the thunderstorm forecast. Draw a thunderstorm. Talk about how to be safe during thunderstorms.

Name: _____

Tornados are made of fast-moving winds. They make a funnel cloud.

funnel cloud

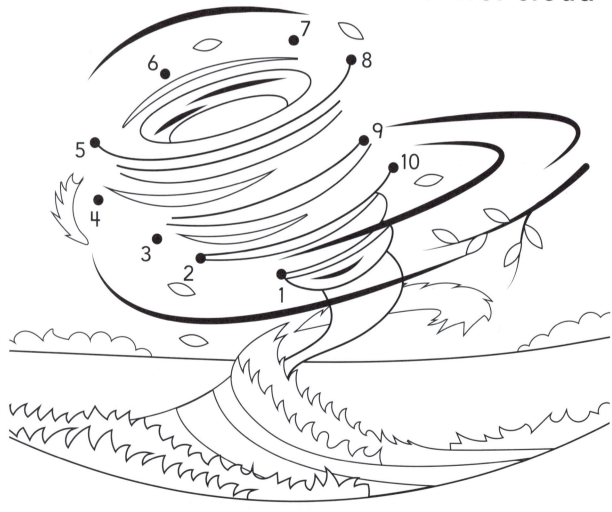

Directions: Read about tornados. Look at the pictures of tornados. Connect the dots to make the picture. Color the picture. Talk about how people might stay safe during tornados.

Name: _____

Hurricanes are large storms. They have strong and fast winds.

Time to Draw

Weather scientists can take pictures from space.

Directions: Read about hurricanes. Look at the pictures of hurricanes. Draw a hurricane-like picture taken from space. Talk about how people might stay safe during a hurricane.

Weather Forecasting

Name: _____

What is a

blizzard?

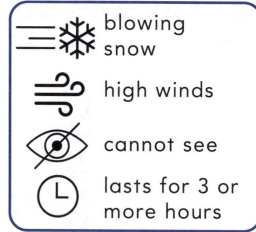

	blowing snow
	high winds
	cannot see
L	lasts for 3 or more hours

Time to Draw

You cannot see in a blizzard because of blowing snow.

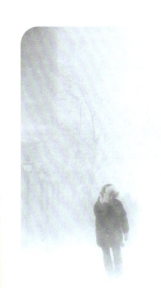

blowing snow

high winds

cannot see

Directions: Read about blizzards. Trace the word *blizzard*. Look at the chart about blizzards. Look at the picture of a blizzard. Draw the symbols next to the words. Talk about how people might stay safe during blizzards. Dance as if you are a blizzard.

Name: _____

Hail is frozen rain. It can be small or big.

Time to Draw

A hailstorm happens when wind blows hail.

Directions: Read about hail. Look at the pictures of hail. Look at the picture of a hailstorm and the hailstorm symbols. Draw your own hailstorm symbol. Talk about how people can stay safe during a hailstorm.

Name: _____

Weather Forecasting

Ice storms are freezing rain. The freezing rain covers things in ice.

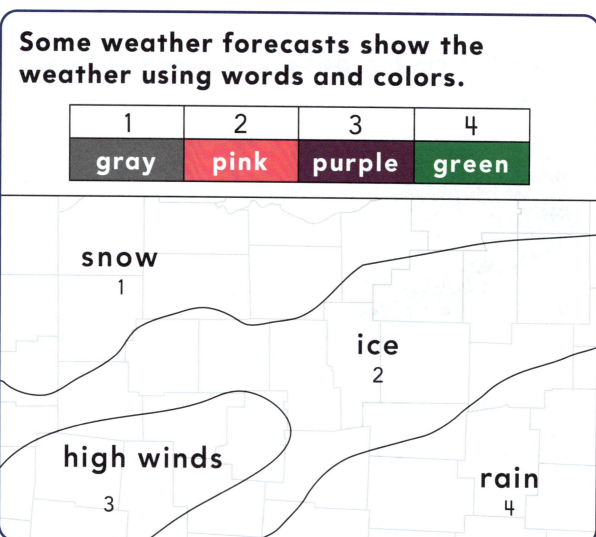

Some weather forecasts show the weather using words and colors.

1	2	3	4
gray	pink	purple	green

snow
1

ice
2

high winds
3

rain
4

Directions: Read about ice storms. Look at the picture of an ice storm. Talk about how people can stay safe during an ice storm. Use the color key to color the weather forecast map.

Kinds of Weather

snow

sun

clouds

storm

rain

wind

Today's Weather	
Morning cold warm hot	
Afternoon cold warm hot	

Weather Forecasting

Directions: Look at the symbols showing different kinds of weather. Color the symbols. Look outside in the morning and afternoon. Draw symbols from the top of the page to show the weather. Circle the temperatures for the morning and afternoon.

Name: _____

Kinds of Weather

snow

sun

clouds

storm

rain

wind

Today's Weather	
Morning cold warm hot	
Afternoon cold warm hot	

Directions: Look at the symbols showing different kinds of weather. Color the symbols. Look outside in the morning and afternoon. Draw symbols from the top of the page to show the weather. Circle the temperatures for the morning and afternoon.

130221—180 Days of Science

Name: _____

To reduce is to use less of something.

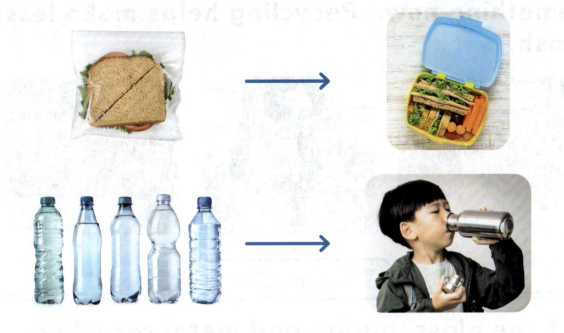

Time to Draw

Directions: Read about reducing. Look at the pictures showing ways to reduce waste. Talk about ways to reduce waste, such as turning off the water when you're not using it and using reusable containers. Draw a way to reduce waste.

Name: _____

To recycle is to remake trash into something new. Recycling helps make less trash.

Reducing Human Impact

Time to Color

I see glass, paper, and metal recycling.

paper   glass   metal

Directions: Read about recycling. Look at the examples of recycling. Find examples of recycling in books or in your community. Color the picture of recycling.

Name: _____

To reuse is to use something again. We can use fewer things if we reuse them.

Which shows reusing?

Which shows reusing?

Directions: Read about reusing. Color the pictures of reused items. Find examples of reusing in books or in your community. Circle the best answers to the questions. Pretend you are grocery shopping using a reusable bag.

Name: _____

You can turn the water off when you brush your teeth. This helps save water.

turn off

Reducing Human Impact

Time to Draw

Directions: Read about saving water. Look at the picture. Talk about how to brush your teeth with the water turned off. Draw yourself brushing your teeth and using less water. Practice brushing your teeth this way.

130221—180 Days of Science

Name: _____

We can catch rainwater and use it later. A rain chain catches water. A rain barrel catches water, too.

rain chain   rain barrel

Time to Draw

I can save rainwater.	I can use saved rainwater.

Directions: Read about saving rainwater. Look at the examples of catching rainwater. Talk about ways to catch rainwater. Draw yourself catching rainwater to use later. Color the picture of using rainwater to water plants.

© Shell Education

130221—180 Days of Science

179

Reducing Human Impact

Name: _____

We can catch water when washing fruits and vegetables. We can water plants with the water we save.

catch water

Which pictures show saving water?

Directions: Read about catching water. Look at the picture of catching water. Circle the pictures that show saving water. Create and sing a song about saving water when washing fruits and vegetables.

Name: _____

Sometimes, we can ride bikes instead of driving cars. This helps keep the air clean. Cars burn gas that makes the air dirty.

Time to Draw

Directions: Read about riding bikes. Look at the picture of riding bikes. Talk about where you can ride a bike and how it helps keep the air clean. Color the picture. Draw yourself riding a bike. Act out riding a bike.

Name: _____

Sometimes, people can ride buses, trains, and subways. This keeps cars off the road. This helps keep the air clean.

Directions: Read about riding buses, trains, and subways. Look at the pictures. Talk about buses, trains, and subways in your community. Color the pictures. If possible, take a ride on a bus, train, or subway in your community with an adult.

Name: _____

Some people drive electric cars. Electric cars do not burn gasoline. This helps keep the air clean.

Time to Draw

My Design

Directions: Read about electric cars. Look at the pictures of electric cars. Talk about electric cars in your community. Design your own electric car. Remember to add where the car will plug in to charge. Talk about your design.

We can plant trees to help keep the air clean. Trees capture things that make the air dirty. We need clean air to breathe.

Time to Draw

Reducing Human Impact

Directions: Read about planting trees. Look at the pictures of people planting trees. Talk about planting trees in your community. Draw four small trees that have just been planted. Draw some birds. Color the picture.

Name: _____

Paper is made from trees. We can reuse paper. We can recycle paper. This will help us cut down fewer trees.

Time to Draw

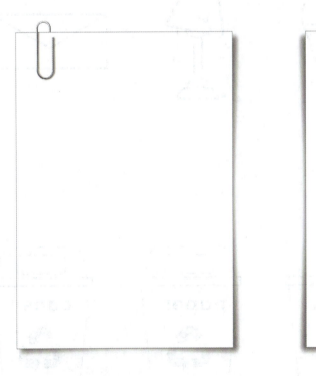

front   back

Directions: Read about reusing and recycling paper. Look at the pictures of making, recycling, and reusing paper. Draw pictures on the front and back of the paper. Reuse and recycle paper when you can.

Name: _____

We can protect the land by putting trash in trash cans. We can recycle paper, glass, and plastic.

Reducing Human Impact

littering

trash cans

recycling

plastic

trash

paper

cans

Directions: Read about trash, littering, and recycling. Look at the pictures. Talk about how trash and recycling bins are used in your community. Draw lines from each piece of trash to the correct bin. Color the picture. Pretend to put trash in bins.

Name: _____

We can help the land by composting. Composting turns waste scraps into soil.

Time to Draw

We can compost leaves and grass. We can compost fruit and vegetable scraps.

Directions: Read about composting and compost bins. Look at the picture of composting. Draw things that you can compost. If possible, talk with your family about composting at home.

Name: _____

Reducing Human Impact

We can use less energy by using natural light from the sun.

I see light from the

sun.

Directions: Read about natural light from the sun. Find natural light in your home or school. Trace the word *sun*. Circle the pictures with natural light.

Name: _____

We can use less energy. We can turn off electronics and lights when we are not using them.

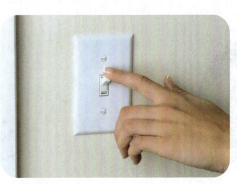

Time to Draw

Directions: Read about turning off electronics and lights. Look at the pictures of turning off electronics and lights. Circle the pictures of electronics being turned off. Draw yourself turning something off.

Name: _____

We can use less air conditioning or heat to save energy. We can dress for the weather when it is hot or cold.

Time to Draw

Reducing Human Impact

Directions: Read about using air conditioning and heat. Look at the pictures. Draw what you could wear on a warm day. Draw what you could wear on a cold day.

Name: _____

You can keep the doors and windows closed when the heat or air conditioning is on. This helps you use less energy.

Time to Draw

Directions: Read about closing windows and doors. Look at the pictures of closed windows and doors. Talk about closing doors and windows to help use less energy. Circle the pictures of closed windows and doors. Draw a closed window.

Name: _____

People can use less energy when they put timers on lights. Timers make lights turn on and off at certain times.

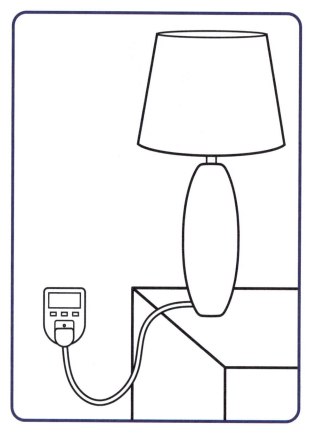

Directions: Read about timers on lights. Look at the pictures of light timers. Color the pictures of lights with timers. Use yellow to make the lights look like they are turned on.

Name: _____

It takes energy to heat water. We can save energy when we use less hot water.

Which picture shows hot water?

Which picture shows cold water?

Which picture shows using less hot water?

Directions: Read about using less hot water. Look at the picture of hot water. Talk about ways to use less hot water. Circle the best answers to the questions. Act out taking a short shower to use less hot water.

Reducing Human Impact

Reducing Human Impact

Name: _____

People can use the sun's energy when they use solar power. Solar power makes electricity using light from the sun.

Time to Draw

Directions: Read about solar power. Look at the pictures of solar panels. Draw solar panels on the roof of the house. Color the picture. Act out being a solar panel that is taking in light from the sun.

Congratulations!
You did it!

Congratulations to:

_____

Achievement:

You worked hard for 180 days to learn science!

Way to go! You did your best!

Awarded by: _____ **Date:** _____

Directions: Read the certificate aloud. Draw yourself learning about science. Post this certificate somewhere special.

Rubric

Directions: This rubric can be used for any open-ended questions where student responses vary. Evaluate student work to determine how many points out of 9 students earn. Discuss answers with the child to ensure understanding. It is developmentally appropriate for children at this level to express ideas with drawings only. In these cases, discuss the child's drawings.

Student Name: _____

	3 Points	**2 Points**	**1 Point**
Content Knowledge	Gives right answer based on content *and* prior knowledge.	Gives right or mostly right answer based on content *or* prior knowledge.	Gives incorrect answer.
Analysis	Thinks about the content and draws correct and strong inferences/conclusions.	Thinks about the content and draws somewhat correct inferences/conclusions.	Thinks about the content but draws incorrect inferences/conclusions.
Explanation	Explains and supports responses with robust evidence.	Explains and supports responses with some evidence.	Provides little or no evidence for responses.

Total: _____

_____

_____

_____

_____

_____

_____

Semester Recording Sheet

Directions: Select days at the beginning and end of each semester to use the Rubric (page 196) to score students' responses. After scoring, record students' scores here. Compare the two scores each semester.

Student Name	S1 Date	S1 Date	S2 Date	S2 Date
1.				
2.				
3.				
4.				
5.				
6.				
7.				
8.				
9.				
10.				
11.				
12.				
13.				
14.				
15.				
16.				
17.				
18.				
19.				
20.				

Trimester Recording Sheet

Directions: Select days at the beginning and end of each trimester to use the Rubric (page 196) to score students' responses. After scoring, record students' scores here. Compare the two scores each trimester.

Student Name	T1 Date	T1 Date	T2 Date	T2 Date	T3 Date	T3 Date
1.						
2.						
3.						
4.						
5.						
6.						
7.						
8.						
9.						
10.						
11.						
12.						
13.						
14.						
15.						
16.						
17.						
18.						
19.						
20.						

Three Strands Recording

Directions: At the beginning and end of each of the three strands of science in this book, use the Rubric (page 196) to score students' responses. After scoring, record students' scores here. Compare the two scores for each of the three strands.

Student Name	Life Science Date	Life Science Date	Physical Science Date	Physical Science Date	Earth and Space Science Date	Earth and Space Science Date
1.						
2.						
3.						
4.						
5.						
6.						
7.						
8.						
9.						
10.						
11.						
12.						
13.						
14.						
15.						
16.						
17.						
18.						
19.						
20.						

References Cited

Byington, Teresa A., and Yaebin Kim. 2017. "Promoting Preschoolers' Emergent Writing." *Young Children* 72 (5). naeyc.org/resources/pubs/yc/ nov2017/emergent-writing.

Duschl, Richard A., Heidi A. Schweingruber, and Andrew W. Shouse, eds. 2007. *Taking Science to School: Learning and Teaching Science in Grades K-8*. Washington, DC: National Academies Press.

First Things First. 2017. "Early Childhood Brain Development Has Lifelong Impact." *Arizona PBS*. azpbs.org/2017/11/early-childhood-brain-development-lifelong-impact/.

Hirsch, Megan. 2010. *How to Hold a Pencil*. Los Angeles: Hirsch Indie Press.

Michaels, Sarah, Andrew W. Shouse, and Heidi A. Schweingrube. 2007. *Ready, Set, Science!* Washington, DC: National Academy Press.

Worth, Karen. 2010. *Science in Early Childhood Classrooms: Content and Process*. Newton, MA: Early Childhood Research and Practice. ecrp.illinois.edu/beyond/seed/worth.html.

Suggested Websites

Website	URL	Content
World Wildlife Fund	www.worldwildlife.org/	reading and videos
NASA Kids Club	www.nasa.gov/kidsclub/index.html	reading, activities and games
Tree People	www.treepeople.org/	reading, videos, and activities
Epic!	www.getepic.com	reading books and videos (subscription)
National Geographic Kids	www.kids.nationalgeographic.com	reading, videos, games
PBS Kids	pbskids.org/apps/	apps, games, and videos
Ology (The American Museum of Natural History)	www.amnh.org/explore/ology	reading books, games, activities, and videos
Little Bins for Little Hands	littlebinsforlittlehands.com/science-experiments-and-activities/	experiments
Energy Kids	www.eia.gov/kids/	activities and experiments
Weather Wiz Kids	www.weatherwizkids.com/	experiments

Answer Key

page 17

seed

seedling

root

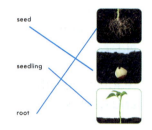

page 32

f	o	o	d	i
j	f	o	o	d
g	c	b	a	z
e	f	o	o	d
f	o	o	d	l

page 38

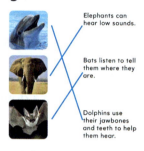

Elephants can hear low sounds.

Bats listen to tell them where they are.

Dolphins use their jawbones and teeth to help them hear.

page 42

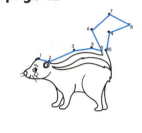

page 25

Are the plants watered?

page 33

Who is drinking?

page 39

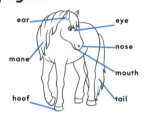

ear

eye

mane

nose

mouth

hoof

tail

page 43

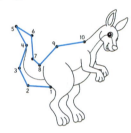

page 28

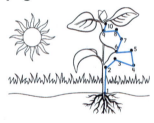

page 34

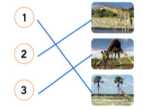

page 40

page 31

Which shows an animal eating food?

Which shows animals drinking water?

page 36

Sharks breathe with their gills.

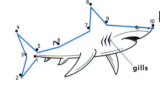

gills

page 41

Answer Key

Answer Key *(cont.)*

page 46
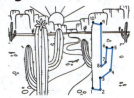

page 57
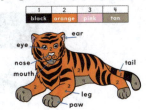

page 61

page 66

page 50
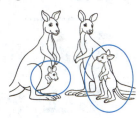

page 58

page 62

page 67
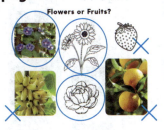

page 52

page 59
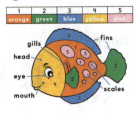

page 63

page 72

page 53

page 60
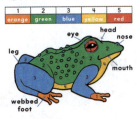

page 64
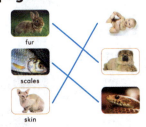

page 74

© Shell Education

130221—180 Days of Science

203

Answer Key *(cont.)*

page 77
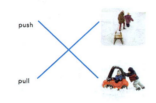

page 89
We can push to stop motion.

page 106
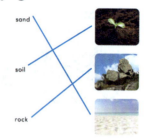

page 121
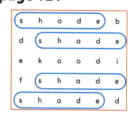

page 79

page 90

page 109

page 123
Shade at the Beach

page 87
pushing a boat

pushing a tractor

pushing a car
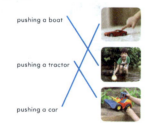

page 92
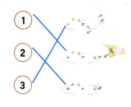

page 112

page 126
Sunlight shines during the day.

page 88
Pushing or Pulling?

page 93
fast

slow
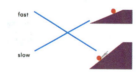

page 113
sun

rain

snow

page 128
When it snows, the temperature is cold.

Answer Key (cont.)

page 130

page 134

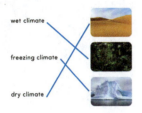

wet climate
freezing climate
dry climate

page 136

page 140

1
2
3

page 141

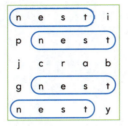

page 146

page 152

page 154

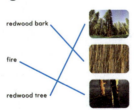

redwood bark
fire
redwood tree

page 158

Where are the tigers?

page 159

camel
ATV
car

page 160

dogsled
truck
snowmobile

page 163

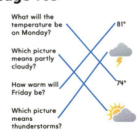

What will the temperature be on Monday?

Which picture means partly cloudy?

How warm will Friday be?

Which picture means thunderstorms?

81°

74°

page 168

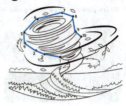

page 170

blowing snow

high winds

cannot see

page 172

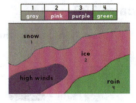

1	2	3	4
gray	pink	purple	green

snow 1
ice 2
high winds
rain 4

page 177

Which shows reusing?

Which shows reusing?

Answer Key (cont.)

page 180

Which pictures show saving water?

page 191

page 186

page 193

Which picture shows hot water?

Which picture shows cold water?

Which picture shows using less hot water?

page 188

I see light from the

page 189

Digital Resources

Accessing the Digital Resources

The digital resources can be downloaded by following these steps:

1. Go to **www.tcmpub.com/digital**

2. Use the ISBN number to redeem the digital resources.

3. Respond to the question using the book.

4. Follow the prompts on the Content Cloud website to sign in or create a new account.

5. The content redeemed will now be on your My Content screen. Click on the product to look through the digital resources. All resources are available for download. Select files can be previewed, opened, and shared.

   For questions and assistance with your ISBN redemption, please contact Shell Education.

   email: customerservice@tcmpub.com
   phone: 800-858-7339

Contents of the Digital Resources

Activities

- Ideas for extending the learning to real-world situations
- Taking Care of Earth Matching Game
- Templates for creating student books about science topics
- Hands-on practice for learning uppercase and lowercase letters
- Writing practice of uppercase and lowercase letters

Teacher Resources

- Certificate of Completion
- Rubric
- Recording Sheets
- Standards Correlations